Melvin Weston Rowell

Privates' Handbook of Military Courtesy and Guard Duty

Melvin Weston Rowell

Privates' Handbook of Military Courtesy and Guard Duty

ISBN/EAN: 9783337280628

Printed in Europe, USA, Canada, Australia, Japan

Cover: Foto ©Lupo / pixelio.de

More available books at **www.hansebooks.com**

Privates' Handbook

OF

MILITARY COURTESY

AND

GUARD DUTY

Being Paragraphs from Authorized Manuals with
Changes in Manual of Arms, Saluting, etc.,
according to Recent Modifications, and
their Adaptations to the Springfield Arm, Embodied,
and Notes.

BY

Lieut. MELVIN W. ROWELL,
United States Army,

Sometime Instructor in Guard Duty and Military Courtesy,
Division, National Guard of New Jersey.

KANSAS CITY, MO.
HUDSON-KIMBERLY PUBLISHING CO.
1898

CONTENTS.

THE POSTING OF A RELIEF.

S', old sentinel; S^2, new sentinel; C', old corporal; C^2, new corporal. *When old corporal $(\underline{C'})$ is not present, there is no change.*

1st Stage.

Sentinel halts when relief is 15 paces away.

```
C²|
    | | | |
    | | | |
      C'|                    |S'
```

2d Stage.

Relief halts at 6 paces; corporal commands "No. (—);" new sentinel advances and halts 1 pace from old sentinel.

```
    | | | |          C²
    | | |        S²| |S'
                    C'
```

3d Stage.

Positions at command "Post," and while relief is passing.

```
            C²
          | | | |
           | | |
        S²  C'  S'
```

4th Stage.

Relief being 6 paces away, new sentinel walks post.

```
        C²|
                      | | | |
                      | | | |
        S²              C'|
```

PREFACE.

The private of the National Guard, or of volunteers, often meeting with doubts and difficulties in referring to unabridged manuals for details, a handbook for his individual guidance is of considerable assistance, if not a necessity, to company commanders in the routine instruction, or quick training of their commands in fundamental duties.

An effort has here been made to place before the soldier in a convenient, compact, and economical form essential features which he must learn not only in order to perform well his present duties, but that, should he later rise to the position of non-commissioned officer or officer, his comprehension of his new duties as a subordinate and as an instructor will rest on a solid foundation. With this object in view, certain paragraphs of authorized manuals and regulations of the United States Army are presented with supplementary paragraphs added (printed in small type) where thought necessary to aid the inexperienced.

On my own responsibility, the changes in the Manual of Arms, saluting, etc., due to recent modifications (also their adaptation to the Springfield arm), have been embodied in the paragraphs from authorized manuals.

Advice and suggestions have been received from Captains B. M. Gerardin, 4th Regiment, and T. D. Landon, 6th Regiment, National Guard of New Jersey, to whom my thanks are returned.

Melvin W. Rowell,

Lieutenant U. S. Army.

Newark, New Jersey, March 10, 1898.

SALUTE WITH HAND.

MILITARY COURTESY.

Saluting.

1.   Courtesy among military men is indispensable to discipline; respect to superiors will not be confined to obedience on duty, but will be extended on all occasions.

Officers and men, when saluting, look toward the person saluted.

Salute with the Hand.

2.   Enlisted men salute with the hand farthest from the officer, giving the salute 6 paces before passing the officer and holding the hand at the visor until the salute is acknowledged or the officer passed.

The salute is made in two motions:

1st.   Raise the hand smartly until the forefinger touches the lower part of the headdress above the right eye, thumb and fingers extended and joined, palm to the left, forearm inclined at about 45 degrees, hand and wrist straight.

2d.   Drop the arm quietly by the side.

If uncovered, the forefinger touches the forehead above the eye.

Rifle Salute.

3.   The rifle salute is prescribed for individual soldiers with arms, except sentinels, who salute by presenting arms.

The first motion of the rifle salute is made 6 yards before passing the officer, holding the hand at the small of the stock until the salute is acknowledged or the officer passed.

The salute is made as below:

Being at a right shoulder—

1st.   Carry the left hand smartly to the small of the stock, forearm horizontal, palm of the hand down, thumb and forefingers extended and joined, forefinger against the piece.

2d.   Drop the left hand by the side.

4.   When indoors, the salute is made from the position of order arms:

1st.   Carry the left hand smartly to the right side, forearm horizontal, or nearly so, palm of the hand down, thumb and fingers extended and joined, forefinger against the piece.

2d.   Drop the left hand by the side.

RIFLE SALUTE.

Honors.

5. Enlisted men passing the uncased color will render the prescribed salute; with no arms in hand, the salute will be made by uncovering.

6. No honors are paid by troops when on the march or in trenches. and no salute is rendered when marching in double time or at the trot or gallop.

7. When an enlisted man without arms passes an officer, he salutes with the hand farthest from the officer. If mounted, he salutes with the right hand. Officers are saluted whether in uniform or not.

8. An enlisted man, on foot and armed with the rifle or carbine, makes the rifle or carbine salute. If armed with the saber and out of ranks, he salutes all officers with the saber if drawn; otherwise he salutes with the hand. A mounted soldier dismounts before addressing an officer not mounted.

9. A non-commissioned officer or private in command of a detachment without arms salutes all officers with the hand; but if the detachment be on foot and armed with the rifle or carbine, he makes the rifle or carbine salute; and if armed with the saber, he salutes with it. *He brings the detachment, if armed, to port arms when at about 30 paces from the officer.*

10. An enlisted man, if seated, rises on the approach of an officer, faces toward him and salutes. If standing, he faces the officer for the same purpose. If the parties remain in the same place or on the same ground, such compliments need not be repeated, *but a correct demeanor will be observed.* Soldiers actually at work do not cease work to salute an officer unless addressed by him. *Soldiers actively engaged in athletic exercises or bathing do not salute passing officers.*

11. An enlisted man makes the prescribed salute with the weapon he is armed with, or if unarmed, whether covered or uncovered, with the hand, before addressing an officer. He also makes the same salute after receiving a reply.

12. Indoors, an unarmed enlisted man uncovers and stands at attention upon the approach of an officer; he does not salute unless he addresses or is addressed by the officer. If armed, he salutes as heretofore prescribed, without uncovering. *A soldier in a tent does not salute a passing officer; he rises and stands at attention.*

13. When an officer enters a room where there are soldiers, the word "Attention" is given by some one who perceives him, when all rise and remain

standing in the position of a soldier until the officer leaves the room, or commands **"At ease."** However, if an officer be already present in the room, notice will not be thus taken of an **officer who** enters, except **he** be senior to the officer present. Soldiers at meals **do not rise.**

14. The interior of a tent, office, **or company quarters not** actually in use for drill is "in **doors"; the** drill-halls **and** corridors of armories **are considered "out doors."**

15. In a camp the **tents and company** street constitute **the** company quarters: **and when.** a commissioned officer enters the quarters, the **non-commissioned officer in** charge, **or** the **first man** who **perceives** him, salutes, giving first the command "Attention," which is executed and maintained by all until the officer leaves the quarters.

16. **In** saluting officers and in their presence generally, **the coat should be** buttoned, the hat squarely set **on, and, if** smoking, the cigar or pipe should be removed **from the mouth.**

17. Abbreviations of **the titles of officers and non-com-** missioned officers are unmilitary. **Enlisted men** address and refer **to** officers by the grade the officer holds, as: "Private Brown **reports to** Lieutenant Jones;" again, Sir, Corporal Smith **reports to the** commanding officer;" again, "The captain directs," etc.

18.   *Soldiers at all times and in all situations pay the same honors and courtesies to officers of other regiments, corps, etc., as to officers of their own regiment, corps, or arm of the service.*

MANUAL OF GUARD DUTY FOR PRIVATES.

Introduction.

1. *Proper instruction and practice in guard duty is not only necessary in itself to the private, but the distinctive and individual nature of the duties and responsibilities of sentinels affording abundant opportunities for the cultivation of habits of self-reliance, faithfulness, vigilance, and other soldierly virtues much desired in the performance of all military duties, brings guard duty into a close and fundamental relation with all other military training and gives great importance to its correct execution.*

2. *A correct knowledge by the private of the fundamental details of guard duty is best imparted during periods of routine training, and must be based on his learning the principles, and their application, of the authorized manual. The private may acquire a knowledge of the duty through individual study and through recruit and company training; the method by training being preferable, for by this method he, while learning, gains confidence and acquires habit through practice. A camp of instruction is the "prov-*

ing-ground" of previous instruction as well the occasion of adding instruction **and attaining habit,** through the actual performance of practical details of duty. Active service with **guard duty as well as with other duties** should be the final **test of all previous instruction and** training.

3. Whatever the method by which **the private is instructed, it is to be emphasized that there is no "short cut" to an** understanding of guard duty; such knowledge can only be acquired through unremitted, **and at** times tedious, efforts **to** master the rules of the Manual of Guard Duty. **It is** further to be observed **that** guard duty can not be correctly **learned, nor properly and** vigilantly performed, when there **is wanting in a command the** quality of subordination to proper authority, **and, on** the **part** of the **private** on guard, the **honest intention** of performing his **duty in a** soldierly manner, **at all times, and whether or not under the eye of an** officer.

4. **The sentinel** on post **is the** representative of his **commanding** officer, and must **be obeyed and respected by all** accordingly. **The** authority of the sentinel **over** all persons, except those **whom** he **recognizes as competent** to give him orders, is always absolute **and** positive, and when necessary to enforce that authority **he is, as a** final resort, justified **in the use of his arms.**

5. *A well-instructed sentinel is one* **who knows** *the* **general orders** *(the very foundation of all guard duty), the* **special orders** *of his own post, and* **who understands the** *following* **details** *:*

1st. *The number, limit, extent, and duties of his post.*

2d. *Whom to allow to cross during the day and whom at night.*

3d. *When to use port arms.*

4th. *When and how to challenge.*

5th. *Whose orders* **are** *received* **and obeyed.**

6th. *The rules of saluting.*

The sentinel learns the **general orders,** *his duties and the details of their performance, from the Manual of Guard Duty, from the commanding* **officer's orders** *posted* **on bulletin-boards** *at the* **guard** *tents, and from verbal orders* **and** *instruction imparted* **by the** *officers and* **non-commissioned** *officers* **of his own guard.**

PRIVATES OF THE GUARD.

1. Without permission from the commander of the guard, members of the guard will not remove their accouterments or clothing, nor leave the immediate vicinity of the guard-house.

2. When not engaged in the performance of a specific duty, a member will salute all officers who pass him. This rule applies at all hours of the day or night.

3. Whenever the guard or relief is dismissed, each member not at once required for duty will place his rifle in the arm-racks, if they be provided, and will not remove it therefrom unless he requires it in the performance of some duty.

4. Privates will not change from one relief or post to another, during the same tour of guard duty, unless by proper authority.

5. Should the guard be formed, soldiers will fall in ranks under arms. *In all cases the* **guard**, *or reliefs, fall in at* **order arms.**

At a roll-call each man, as his name, number, and relief are called, answers "**Here**," and comes to order arms.

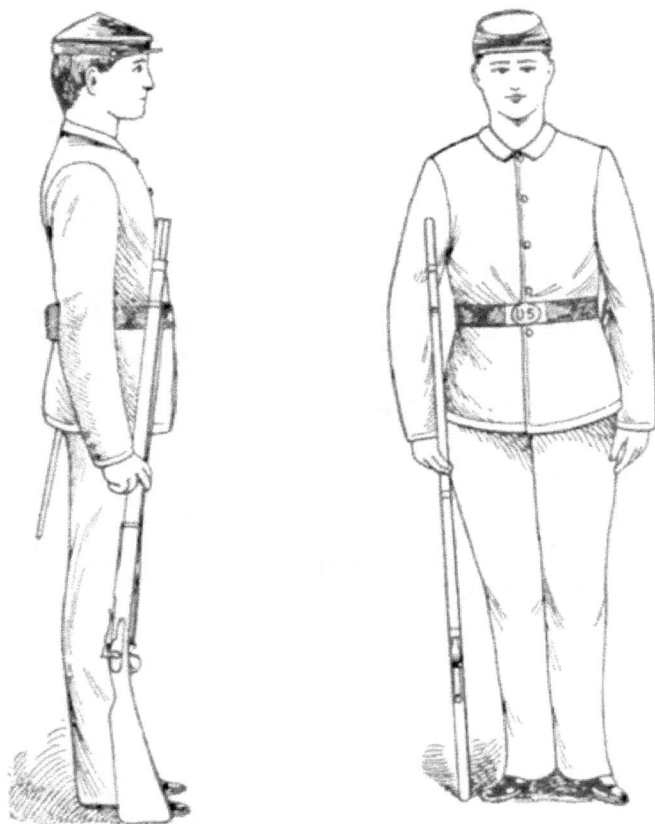

ORDER ARMS.

Should No. 1 call **"The guard,"** *or* **"Turn out the guard,"** *etc., each private makes an effort to get into ranks with his rifle, quickly—i. e., with a rush.*

6. No soldier shall hire another to do his duty for him.

ORDERS FOR ALL SENTINELS ON POST.

7. *The post of a sentinel is usually established in length by certain terminals and the sentinel usually walks the "center two-thirds" of the line; but sentinels should remember that the extent of their post and the field of their vigilant observation is not limited to such a path, and that they may go to a reasonable distance to either side when necessary to perform the duties for which they are posted. A sentinel may even go to the assistance of an adjoining sentinel who is being overpowered, or who is disabled, provided the duties of his own post are not thereby neglected. The sentinel is expected to, first, last, and all the time, be vigilant and to use his common sense.*

8. When calling for any purpose, challenging, or in communication with any person, an infantry sentinel will take the position of **port arms**. *This rule is important; the infantry sentinel on post, whenever he opens his mouth to speak, and whenever spoken to, comes to port* **arms.** A cavalry sentinel, if dismounted, will take the position of **port arms, raise pistol,** or **port saber,** according as he is armed with the carbine, pistol, or saber; if mounted, he will take the position of advance

PORT ARMS.

carbine, **raise pistol**, or guard; he will **not dismount without** authority, **while** on duty **as a sentinel.**

9. **A sentinel will not quit** his **piece**, except on an explicit order from some person from whom he **lawfully** receives orders while on post; under no circumstances **will he yield it to any** other person.

10. A sentinel **will** arrest suspicious persons prowling about **the post or camp at** any time, **all parties** to a disorder occurring on or **near his post,** or **any** one who attempts **to enter the camp at night,** even soldiers of other corps, and will **turn over all persons** arrested **to the corporal of the guard.** *To arrest a person the sentinel keeps* **him in** *place, ordering him not to move, but to remain where he is standing, using force if necessary,* **calls a** *corporal of the guard, and upon his arrival explains the circumstances and turns over the person held.*

11. He **will at once report** to the **corporal of** the **guard** every unusual **or** suspicious **event noticed.** *A sentinel, as a rule,* **does not permit soldiers or others to** *loiter or assemble on or* **near his post or the adjacent** *sentry-boxes.*

12. Orders for **sentinels on post are divided into two classes, general orders and special orders.**

13. Sentinels **will be** required **to memorize the** following:

My general orders are:

To take charge of this post and all Government property in view;

To walk my post in a military manner, keeping constantly on the alert, observing everything that takes place within sight or hearing;

To report every breach of orders or regulations that I am instructed to enforce;

To repeat all calls from posts more distant from the guard-house than my own;

To quit my post only when properly relieved;

To receive, transmit, and obey all orders from, and allow myself to be relieved by the commanding officer, officer of the day, an officer or non-commissioned officer of the guard only;

To hold conversation with no one except in the proper discharge of my duty;

In case of fire or disorder, to give the alarm;

To allow no one to commit nuisance in the vicinity of my post;

In any case not covered by instructions, to call the corporal of the guard;

To salute all officers, and colors or standards not cased;

At night to exercise the greatest vigilance. **Between**
... **o'clock** *(this hour is designated by the commanding officer)* and **broad** daylight, **challenge all persons seen on or**
near **my post, and** allow **no person to pass without proper**
authority.

14. *It is seen that the sentinel obeys the* **orders** *of certain*
officers and non-commissioned officers only. *While any offi-*
cer has **the right** *to call the attention of a private of the* **guard**
or of a sentinel to any matter of duty, **only** *such officers* **and**
non-commissioned officers as have authority over, or with, *the*
guard can give him orders.   This **rule in no** *way detracts*
from the respect due all officers.

15. **Special orders** define the duties to be performed
by a sentinel **on** a particular post, **and** are prescribed by
the commanding officer.   *That the sentinel may learn*
them, they are usually posted on bulletin-boards at the **guard-**
tents and in **the** *sentry-boxes.*

The sentinel **at the commanding officer's tent will**
warn **him, day or night, of any unusual movement in**
or about **the camp.**

16. Whenever relieved, a sentinel will repeat, **in**
detail, to his successor, all special orders relating to
his post.

17. A sentinel on post is not required to halt and
change the position of his rifle on arriving at the end

of his post, nor to execute **to the rear march**, precisely as prescribed in the Drill Regulations, but faces about **while marching** in the way most convenient to him, *without regard to the position of adjacent sentinels*, and either to the right about or left about, and at any part of his post, as may be best suited to the proper performance of his duties.

He carries his rifle on either shoulder, and at night, or in wet and severe weather, when not in the sentry-box, he may carry it at a secure.

*A sentinel **is not** allowed to stand on post, to converse with an adjacent **sentinel**, or carry the rifle otherwise than as **pre-cribed**; such "slouching" on post is not only unsoldierly, but it does **not** permit that vigilance which is **the distinguishing feature** of guard **duty**. At night and in rainy weather vigilance **is not** to be relaxed, but rather redoubled.*

18. Sentinels, when in sentry-boxes, stand **at ease.** Sentry-boxes will be used in wet weather only.

19. If relief become necessary, by reason of sickness or other cause, the sentinel will call, "**Corporal of the Guard, No. (—); relief,**" giving the number of his post.

20. To call a corporal of the guard for any other purpose than for relief, the sentinel will call, "**Corporal of the Guard, No. (—).**"

RIGHT SHOULDER.

SECURE ARMS.

21. *Sentinels must not call a* **corporal** *of the* **guard except** *by reason of duty. The useless calling of a corporal* **for such** *details as a well-instructed, thoughtful sentinel could* **himself** *perform* **is not** *conducive* **to a** *manly, self-reliant, intelligent,* and **proper** *performance* **of guard** *duty.*

22. **If a sentinel is to be relieved, he will halt** and **face toward the relief with arms at right shoulder** when the **relief is 15 paces from him.** *The relief is halted about 6 paces from him; the sentinel taking post at the corporal's command* **"No. (—),"** *advances at right shoulder and halts 1 pace from him, when both sentinels come to* **port arms.** The old sentinel, **under the supervision of both** corporals, **gives in a low tone his instructions to the one** taking post. **At the command "Post,"** both sentinels then **resume** the right shoulder, face toward the **new** corporal, and **step back** so as to allow **the relief to pass** in front of **them. The old sentinel takes his** place **in** rear of the **relief as it passes him, his piece in the** same position as those **of the relief. The new** sentinel remains **at a** right **shoulder until the relief has** passed **6** paces beyond him, **when he walks to his post.**

23. **Between** ...... *o'clock* **(the hour designated** by **the commanding officer) and broad daylight, if the sentinel sees any person or party on or near his post, he will advance rapidly** *along* his **post toward such person**

or party, and when within about 30 paces will challenge sharply, "Halt. **Who** is there?" · He will place
himself in the best position to receive or, if necessary,
arrest the person or party. *See Pars. 36, 37, 38.*

24. In case a mounted party be challenged, the
sentinel will call, **"Dismount,"** after challenging.

25. A sentinel will not divulge the countersign to
any one except the sentinel who relieves him, or to a
person from whom he properly receives orders, on such
person's verbal order given personally.

 "Any person belonging to the armies of the United
States, who makes known the watchword to any person
not entitled to receive it, according to the rules and
discipline of war, or presumes to give a parole or watchword different from that which he received, shall
suffer death, or such punishment as court-martial may
direct."—*Forty-fourth Article of War.*

ORDERS FOR ALL SENTINELS EXCEPT No. 1.

---

26. In case **of fire, the** sentinel will call, "Fire, **No. (—),"** giving the number of his post; if possible, he **will** extinguish the **fire by his own efforts.** In case of disorder, he will call, **"The Guard, No. (—)."**

If the danger be great, **he will,** in either **case, dis-charge his piece** before calling. *Whenever a sentinel gives an alarm by discharging* **his piece, he** *invariably* **fires straight up** *into the air above his head.*

Night Orders.

27. Until duly recognized, **by countersign or other-**wise, the sentinel will allow no one to approach nearer than about **10 feet from** him.

The sentinel takes **the position of port arms** *(Par. 8) in challenging; a convenient position* **of the rifle, inasmuch as** *the bayonet can readily be brought* **against** *the breast* **of** *a party attempting to force* **him, or in** *case of need the piece can easily* **be brought** *to the* **shoulder** *to aim and fire.* In all *cases, the sentinel is allowed a reasonable latitude on the score* **of** *safety;* **it is correct not to** *allow* **a** *person* **to approach** *nearer than* **10 feet for recognition without** *first bringing the* *rifle to* **charge bayonet, guard,** *or to a like position admitting the effective use of the bayonet.*

28.   The sentinel will suffer one only of any party to approach him for the purpose of giving the countersign, or, if no countersign be used, of being duly recognized.   When this has been done, the whole party is advanced—*i. e.,* allowed to **pass.**

29.   In all cases the sentinel must satisfy himself beyond a reasonable doubt that the parties are what they represent themselves to be, and have a right to pass.   If he be not satisfied, he must cause them to stand, and call the corporal of the guard.   So, likewise, if he have no authority to pass persons with the countersign, or when the party challenged has not the countersign, or gives an incorrect one.

30.   *The authority of* **the sentinel** *to hold any person whom he does not recognize, whoever that person may claim to be,* **is** *absolute.   Although giving* **the** *countersign, persons* **whose** *authority to pass is in reasonable doubt should* **not** *be allowed to pass* **without** *the authority* **of the** *corporal of the guard after proper investigation;* **the corporal** *should take to his next* **superior** *any case that he* **is not competent to** *decide.*

31.   The sentinel will never allow himself to be surprised, nor permit two parties to advance upon him at the same time.

CHARGE BAYONET.

32. If two or more parties approach a sentinel's post from different directions at the same time, all such parties are challenged—*i. e., halted,* in turn. The senior is first advanced in accordance with rules. *See Pars. 36, 37, 38.*

33. If a party be already advanced, and in communication with a sentinel, the latter will challenge any other party that may approach; if the party challenged be senior to the one already on his post, the sentinel will advance such party at once. The senior, if competent to give orders to the sentinel, may direct him to advance any or all of the other parties. *When so directed, the sentinel advances* them *according to the rules.* Without such direction, the sentinel will not advance any of them until the senior leaves him. He will then advance the senior only of the remaining parties, and so on.

34. The following order of rank will govern a sentinel in advancing different persons or parties approaching his post at night: *General officer,* commanding officer, officer of the day, officer of the guard, officers, patrols, non-commissioned officers of the guard in the order of rank, friends.

35. After challenging and duly recognizing an officer, the sentinel, unless spoken to, salutes, and resumes

walking his post; if spoken to, he continues at **port arms**, and salutes when the officer leaves him.

36. If a person having the countersign approach alone, he is advanced to give the countersign.   *Example:*

"**Halt. Who is there?**"   *Answer,* "**Friend with the** countersign (*or* **officer of the day,** *or* **corporal of the guard,** *or* **etc.**)"; *the sentinel will say,* "**Advance friend** (*or* **officer of the day,** *or* **corporal of the guard,** *or* etc.) **with the** countersign"; *and then, the countersign being given,* "**Advance friend** (*or* **officer of the day,** *or* corporal of the **guard,** *or* etc.)."   *See Pars. 23, 24.*

37. When two or more persons approach in one party, the sentinel, on receiving an answer that some one in the party has the countersign, will *invariably* say, "**Advance one with the** countersign," and, if the countersign be given correctly, will then say, "Advance (**so and so**)," repeating the answer to his challenge.   *Example:*

"Halt. **Who is there?**"   *Answer,* "Friends **with the** countersign (*or* **relief,** *or* **etc.**)"; *the sentinel will say,* "**Advance one with the countersign**"; *then,* "Advance friends (*or* **relief,** *or* etc.)."   *See Pars. 23, 24.*

38. If no countersign be **used, the rules** for challenging are the same. The **rules** for advancing are

modified only as follows: Instead of saying, "Advance **(so and so)** with the countersign," the **sentinel will say,** "**Advance (so and so) to** be recognized." Upon recognition the sentinel will say, "Advance (so **and** so)." *Examples:*

"**Halt. Who is there?**" *Answer,* "**Officer of the guard**"; *the sentinel will say,* "**Advance officer of the guard, to be recognized**"; *then, upon recognition,* "**Advance** officer of the guard."

"Halt. **Who is there?**" *Answer,* "**Officer of the day** with friends"; *the sentinel will say,* "**Advance one to be recognized**"; *then, upon recognition,* "**Advance officer of the day** and friends." *See Pars. 23, 24.*

39. *As a rule, written passes* **are never good across sentinels' posts at night; such passes are easily forged, and at night are not legible.**

ORDERS FOR SENTINEL No. 1.
(At the Post of the Guard.)

———

40. Sentinels posted at the guard-house or guard-tent will be required to memorize the following:

Between reveille and retreat, to turn out the guard for all persons entitled to the compliment, for all colors or standards not cased, and for all armed parties approaching my post, except troops at drill, and reliefs or detachments of the guard.

At night, after challenging any person or party, to advance no one, but call the corporal of the guard, repeating the answer to the challenge.

Sentinel No. 1 is also required to memorize Par. 13.

41. *The following are entitled, between reveille and retreat, to have the guard turned out:*

Governor of the State, General Officers, **Command-**ing Officer of the **post or camp,** Officer of **the Day.** *(For others, see Par. 252, Manual of Guard Duty.)*

42. *Examples of No. 1's turning out the guard:*

Upon their approach within convenient hearing distance, No. 1 shouts loudly, **"Turn out the guard, commanding offi-**

cer," *or* "Turn **out** the guard, **Governor of the State,**" *or* "Turn out the guard, national colors," *or* "**Turn out the guard, armed party,**" *or* "etc.," *as the case may be.*

At the **approach of the new** guard at guard **mounting,** the **sentinel will call,** as in the **last example:** "**Turn out the guard, armed** party."

43. Should the person named by **the** sentinel **not** desire the guard formed, he **will** salute **and say,** "Never mind the guard," whereupon **the sentinel** calls, "Never mind the guard." *No. 1 salutes* **all persons** *entitled thereto just like any other* **sentinel.**

44. After having called, "**Turn out the guard,**" the sentinel will **not, in any** case, **call, "Never mind the** guard," **on the** approach **of an armed** party.

45. Though the guard be already formed, he **will not fail to call, "Turn out** the guard," as required **in his** general orders, **except** as provided in Par. 46.

46. If **two or more persons** entitled **to the** compliment approach at the same **time, the sentinel** will call for the senior **only; if the senior does** not desire the guard formed, **the sentinel then** calls, "Never mind the **guard."** The guard will not be turned out for **an officer while a senior entitled to the compliment is at or coming to the post of** the guard.

47.   The sentinels at the post of the guard will warn the commander of the approach of any armed body, and to arrest all suspicious or disorderly persons. They will not permit enlisted men to pass without *their* reporting, *at the guard-tent*, unless orders to the contrary have been given by the commanding officer.

48.   From reveille until retreat is the interval between the firing of the morning and the evening gun; or, if no gun be fired, it is the interval between the sounding of the first note of the reveille, or the first march, if marches be played, and the last note of the retreat.

49.   *Between retreat and the hour designated by the commanding officer for challenging to commence, also between broad daylight and reveille, the sentinel usually informs the corporal of the guard of the approach of any person, party, etc., entitled, during the proper hours, to have the guard turned out.*

50.   In case of fire or disorder in the vicinity of the guard-house, the sentinel posted there will call the corporal of the guard and report the facts to him.

Night Orders.

51. After receiving an answer to his challenge, the sentinel calls, **"Corporal of the guard,** (so and so),**"** repeating the answer to his challenge. He does not in such cases repeat the number of his post. *See Pars. 23, 24.*

52. He remains in the position assumed in challenging until the corporal of the guard advances the person challenged to give the countersign or for recognition, when he resumes walking his post, or, if the party be entitled thereto, he salutes, and, as soon as the salute is acknowledged, resumes walking his post.

53. *The post of No. 1, at the post of the guard, is most important and the duties of the sentinel are of necessity more various than is the case on other posts, even requiring that the most intelligent sentinels be here posted.* **By reason of the** *greater vigilance demanded by the importance* **and variety of** *the duties, the method of challenging* **and** *advancing here at the post of the guard* **differs from all other posts.** *Sentinel* **No. 1 does** *all challenging,* **a corporal of the** *guard (one is* **always on the alert at the guard-tent) does** *all advancing.* **No. 1 detects all who approach his** *post* **or** *the guard-tents, from within* **as well as from** *without the camp, challenges, and then quickly* **calls the corporal of the guard,** *repeating the*

answer to his *challenge, so giving the corporal* **notice** *of the* *presence* **of** *the party. The corporal promptly responds* **to** *each call,* **thus leaving No. 1 free** *to resume his watch. That* *this may be done well, quickly, and without confusion,* **re-** *quires* **careful** *learning* **of their** *respective* **duties** *by No. 1* *and the* **corporal. Examples:**

No. 1 challenges, **"Halt. Who is there?"** *Answer,* **"Friends."** *No. 1 at once calls,* **"Corporal of the guard; friends."** *The corporal at once (briskly advancing toward the party) says,* **"Advance one to be recognized,"** *whereupon No. 1 resumes walking his post. The corporal upon rcogniz- ing the party says,* **"Advance friends."** *So also for* **relief, patrol, etc.**

No. 1, **"Halt. Who is there?"** *Answer,* **"Corporal of the guard."** *No. 1 at once calls,* **"Corporal of the guard; cor- poral of the guard."** *The corporal on the alert then says, advancing as before,* **"Advance corporal of the guard to be recognized";** *and then,* **"Advance corporal of the guard."** *So likewise for* **officer of the day, officer** *of the guard,* **friend, etc.**

COMPLIMENTS FROM ALL SENTINELS.

———

54. Saluting distance is the limit within which individuals and the insignia of rank can be readily recognized; it is assumed to be about 30 paces. *Officers are saluted by night as well as by day.*

55. The salute by sentinels will be made by presenting arms; to salute, the sentinel halts, brings his piece to right shoulder arms, if not already there, and faces outward as the person or party entitled to salute arrives within about 30 paces.

If the officer approaches along the post, the present will be given when the officer arrives at a distance of about 6 yards. If he passes in front of the sentinel, but not along the post, he is saluted just before he passes the sentinel's front. If he cross the post, *from either front or rear* he is saluted just before he crosses.

The sentinel will remain at the present until his salute is returned, or until the person saluted has passed.

If the officer passes along in rear of his post, he is not saluted, but the sentinel stands facing outward until the officer has passed.

A sentinel at port arms, engaged in conversation, executes present arms directly from the position of port arms.

A sentinel in a sentry-box, upon approach of an officer, will stand at an order and present arms therefrom as the officer passes.

A cavalry or artillery sentinel with the saber drawn, whether mounted or dismounted, will salute with the present; when mounted and armed with the carbine, he will advance carbine.

In other cases the sentinel will salute with the hand.

56. The same rules apply when a color or standard not cased, carried by a color guard or armed party, or when the officer commanding a party, whether armed or unarmed, passes; so also when the remains of a deceased officer or soldier are carried past.

57. In case of the approach of an armed party of the guard, the sentinel will halt when it is about 15 paces from him, facing toward the party, with his piece at right shoulder. If not himself relieved, he will, as the party passes, place himself so that it will pass in front of him; he resumes walking his post when the party has passed 6 paces beyond him.

The same rules apply in the case of the approach of the new or old guard.

SALUTE OF SENTINEL.

58. Sentinels will not salute, nor halt on the approach of any armed or unarmed party of troops, except as provided in Par. 57. In any case, if the party be commanded by a commissioned officer, the sentinel will salute him as prescribed in Par. 55.

59. On the approach of an officer from whom he properly receives orders, a sentinel will walk his post toward the officer, and will salute as prescribed in Par. 55; if spoken to, he will face toward the officer, his piece at port arms; he salutes when the officer leaves him.

The same will be observed on the approach of a non-commissioned officer of the guard, except that the sentinel does not salute.

60. An officer is entitled to the compliments prescribed, whether in uniform or not.

61. If an officer or group of officers remain on or near a sentinel's post, the sentinel salutes but once. *Having saluted, the sentinel resumes walking his post, with his rifle in usual position.*

62. A sentinel at port arms, and in communication with an officer, *who is senior*, will not interrupt the communication to salute a junior, unless directed by the senior to do so.

SPECIAL ORDERS FOR SENTINELS IN CHARGE OF PRISONERS.

For Sentinels at the Guard-House.

63. The sentinel at the post of the guard has charge of the prisoners. He will allow none to escape or to cross his post except under proper guard.

He will allow no one to communicate in any way with prisoners without permission from proper authority.

He will at once report to the corporal of the guard any suspicious noise made by prisoners.

He must be prepared to tell, whenever asked, how many prisoners are in the guard-house, and how many are at work, or elsewhere.

Whenever prisoners pass his post, returning from work, he will call the corporal of the guard, notifying him of the number of prisoners so returning. Thus: "Corporal of the guard, (so many) prisoners."

If a prisoner attempts to escape, the sentinel will call, "Halt." If he fails to halt when the sentinel has once repeated his call, and if there be no other possible means of preventing his escape, the sentinel will fire upon him. A sentinel does not use more force than is necessary to prevent the escape, but if the prisoner, having twice been ordered to halt, continues his flight, the sentinel may maim or kill him, and it is his duty to do so.

For Sentinels in Charge of Prisoners at Work.

64. A sentinel in charge of prisoners at work will not suffer them to escape, nor allow them to converse with each other, nor with any person without permission from proper authority. He will not himself speak to them, except in the execution of his duty. He will see that they do not straggle and are orderly in deportment, and that they keep constantly at work.

He will keep his prisoners constantly in front of him, and never allow them to walk at his side or in his rear. He will not at any time lose sight of them. When an officer approaches, or when he approaches an officer within 6 paces, he will salute with the rifle salute, taking care to keep his prisoners constantly in front of him. (A prisoner under charge of a sentinel will not salute an officer.)

In crossing the post of the sentinel at the guardhouse, a sentinel in charge of prisoners will call, "No. 1, (so many) prisoners."

The duties of sentinels, in case prisoners attempt to escape, are explained in Par. 63.

ORDERLY FOR THE COMMANDING OFFICER.

65. When directed by the commander of the guard to fall out and report, the orderly will give his name, company, and regiment to the sergeant of the guard, and, leaving his rifle in the arm-rack in his company quarters, will proceed at once to the commanding officer, reporting: "Sir, Private . . . ., Company . . ., reports as orderly."

66. If the orderly selected be a cavalryman, he will report equipped with saber-belt and saber, unless otherwise directed by the commanding officer, first leaving his carbine in the arm-rack of his troop quarters.

67. In the field, or on the march, the equipment of the orderly will be as directed by the commanding officer.

68. The orderly, while on duty as such, is subject to the orders of the commanding officer only.

69. When ordered to carry a message, he will be careful to deliver it exactly as it was given him.

70. The orderly may be permitted to sleep in his company quarters, or in such other place as the commanding officer may direct.

71. His tour of duty ends when he is relieved by the orderly selected from the guard relieving his own.

72. The orderly is a member of the guard, and his name, company, and regiment are entered on the guard report and lists of the guard.

MUSICIANS OF THE GUARD.

73. Musicians of the guard are subject to the orders of none but the commanding officer, the officer of the day, officers, and non-commissioned officers of the guard.

74. Unless otherwise directed by the commanding officer, they will remain at the guard-house during their tour, and will fall in with the guard when formed. They form on a line with the front rank of the guard, their left 3 paces from the right guide.

75. Musicians of the guard sleep at the guard-house, unless otherwise directed by the commanding officer.

76. They will sound all calls prescribed by the commanding officer, and such other calls as may be ordered by proper authority, at such times and places as may be directed.

77.   Should the guard be turned out for national or regimental colors or standards, the field music of the guard will, when the guard presents arms, sound, **"To the color,"** or **"To the standard,"** or, if any person be entitled thereto, the prescribed march, flourishes, or ruffles, as follows:

The Governor of the State: The General's March.

A Major-General: two flourishes or two ruffles.   A Brigadier General: one flourish or one ruffle.

(For others, see Par. 181, Manual of Guard Duty.)

HORSES, SADDLES, AND BRIDLES, by Major William H. Carter, Assistant Adjutant-General, U. S. A. This book has been officially adopted by the War Department as a standard in the examination of officers of the Regular Army. The author in this volume has endeavored to find and bring together in an available form some of the facts regarded as of value to those upon whom the Government must depend, to a great extent, for important services when war comes upon the country. Full cloth, 368 pages, illustrated; price, $2.75.

QUESTIONS IN ORGANIZATION AND TACTICS, by Lieutenant-Colonel A. L. Wagner, Assistant Adjutant-General, U. S. A. Price, 25 c.

ENGLISH-SPANISH POCKET MANUAL, for the use of forces operating in the field on reconnaissance and other duties. Prepared by Lieutenant R. G. Hill, 20th Infantry, U. S. A. Vest pocket size, cloth, 75c.

MANUAL FOR CYCLISTS, by Captain Howard A. Giddings, Brigadier Signal Officer Connecticut National Guard. Prepared for the use of the Regular Army, Organized Militia, and Volunteer Troops. Full blue cloth, illustrated, 75c.

A FIELD MESSAGE BOOK, for the use of Signalists and Army Officers in the Field. Designed by Major Howard A. Giddings, Brigade Signal Office, Connecticut National Guard. Cipher disk, pencil, blanks, transfer sheets, and filing pockets; all in a compact waterproof cover. Postpaid, $1.00.

JOMINI'S LIFE OF NAPOLEON, in two octavo volumes of more than 600 pages each, with superb atlas of 60 maps, illustrating the various battles and theatres of operations. This edition is limited. Printed from new, clean type, $12.00.

SHELBY AND HIS MEN; OR, THE WAR IN THE WEST, by John N. Edwards. Full cloth bound, 450 pages, postpaid, $1.50.

MILITARY **TOPOGRAPHY AND SKETCHING**; a Revised Edition, prepared for the use of the Department of Engineering. United States Infantry and Cavalry **School of Fort** Leavenworth, **by** Lieut. Edwin A. **Root.** 280 pages, full cloth, $2.50.

CAVALRY **vs. INFANTRY, and** Other Essays. By **Captain F. N. Maude,** R.E. **1 volume, 8vo,** handsomely bound **in blue cloth,** postpaid, $1.50.

THE CONDUCT OF WAR. **By** Lieut.-General **von der Goltz, Prus**sian Army. Full **blue** cloth, $2.00.

MILITARY MAP-READING, FIELD, OUTPOST **AND ROAD** SKETCHING, by Captain W. D. Beach, Instructor **in** Military Topography **at** the U. **S.** Infantry and **Cavalry School.** 124 pages, full cloth, 75 cents.

DICKMAN'S FIELD HOLDER, with blanks **for Road and Posi**tion Sketching **on Practice** Marches, Advance and Rear **Guard** Duty, Outposts, Relay **Lines,** and with Instructions for the **Men** in the Duties of Orderlies and Messengers. Price, 75c; **additional Books** or Fillers, **25c.**

THE WAR GAME SIMPLIFIED, **after the** method **of General Verdy du Vernois.** Designed for use of beginners, **as well as** advanced study of the military art. **Published with** full-sized **maps and** complete apparatus for **conducting an** exercise of the three **arms combined.** Translation **and** arrangement are the work of Captain **Eben Swift, Fifth** Cavalry, formerly **in** charge of the **War Game at the U.** S. Infantry and Cavalry School. Price, $5.00.

INFANTRY FIRE; Its Use **in** Battle. **By Jos. B. Bachelor, Jr., First Lieutenant** Twenty-fourth **United** States Infantry. Handsomely bound **in** leather and complete **with tables** and illustrations. Postpaid, $2.00.

MILITARY LETTERS AND ESSAYS. By Captain F. N. Maude, R.E., author of "Letters on Tactics and Organization," "The Evolution of Modern Drill-Books," Etc. 1 volume, 8vo, handsomely bound in blue cloth. Sent postpaid on receipt of $1.50.

CAVALRY STUDIES FROM TWO GREAT WARS, comprising the French Cavalry in 1870, by Lieutenant-Colonel Bonie (French Army). The German Cavalry in the Battle of Vionville—Mars-La-Tour, by Major Kaehler (German General Staff). The Operations of the Cavalry in the Gettysburg Campaign, by Lieutenant-Colonel George B. Davis, U. S. A. Illustrated; full blue cloth. Sent postpaid on receipt of $1.50.

TACTICAL STUDIES ON THE BATTLES AROUND PLEVNA. By Thilo von Trotha, Captain of the Grenadier Regiment Frederick William IV. (Attached). 1 volume, 8vo, handsomely bound in blue cloth. Sent postpaid on receipt of $1.50.

EXTRACTS FROM AN INFANTRY CAPTAIN'S JOURNAL ON THE TRIAL OF A METHOD FOR EFFECTIVELY TRAINING A COMPANY IN SKIRMISHING AND OUT-POST DUTY, by Major von Arnim, of Hohenzollern Fusilier Regiment No. 40; translated by Major C. J. East, 41st Regiment, D. A. Q. M. G. Full blue cloth, $1.50.